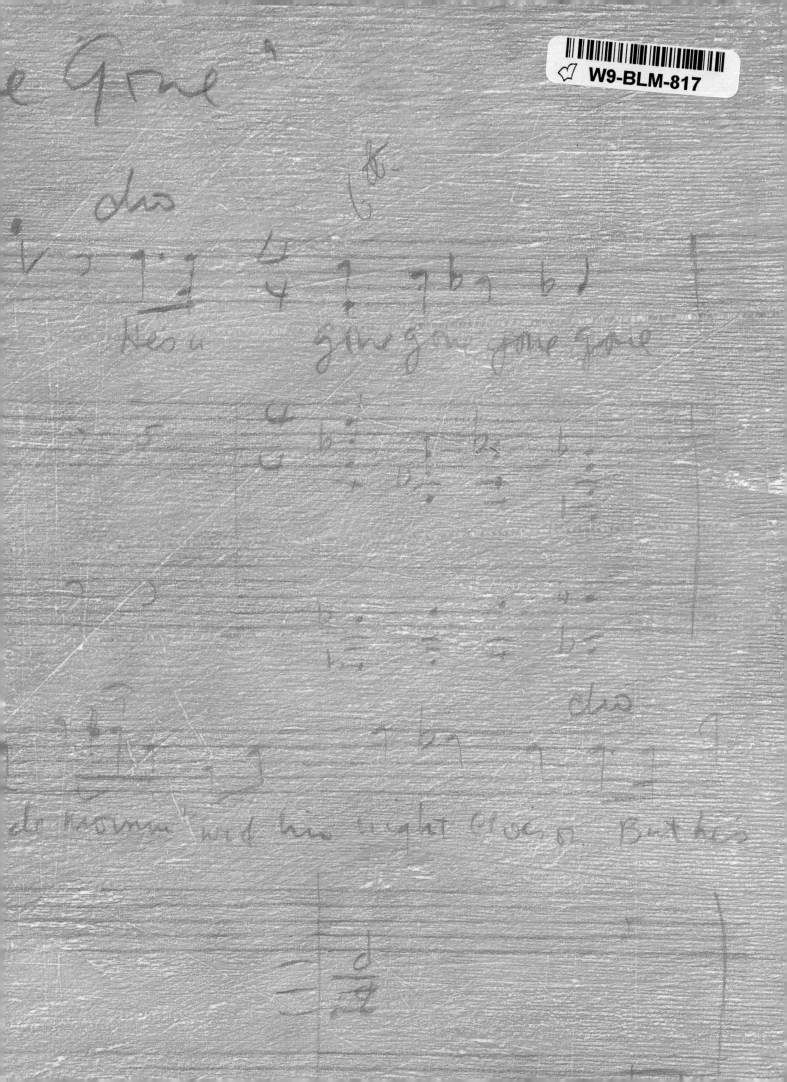

Introducing
GERSHWIN

ROLAND VERNON

Chelsea House Publishers
Philadelphia

SWANEE

WORDS BY I. CAESAR MUSIC BY GEORGE GERSHWIN

JB
GERSHWIN

First published in hardback edition in 2001
by Chelsea House Publishers, a subsidiary of
Haights Cross Communications. All rights reserved.
Printed and bound in China.

First published in the UK in 1996 by
Belitha Press Limited, London House,
Great Eastern Wharf, Parkgate Road,
London SW11 4NQ, England

Text copyright © Roland Vernon 1996
Illustrators copyright © Ian Andrew 1996

Editor: Claire Edwards
Designer: Wilson Design Associates
Picture Researcher: Juliet Duff and Diana Morris

First printing
1 3 5 7 9 8 6 4 2

The Chelsea House World Wide Web address is
http://www.chelseahouse.com

Library of Congress Cataloging-in-Publication Data applied for.

ISBN: 0-7910-6040-3

Picture acknowledgments:
Associated Press/Wide World: 21 Top.
Bridgeman Art Library: 12 left Private Collection.
Donald Cooper/Phototstage: 27 top.
Culver Pictures Inc: title page, back cover, 6 bottom, 10 top, 10 bottom left,
10 bottom right, 12 right, 15 top, 19 bottom, 22 top, 22 bottom.
E.T. Archive: 16 top.
Mary Evans Picture Library: 20 bottom.
Ronald Grant Archive: 19 top, 20 top, 28 top.
Robert Harding Picture Library: 7 top, 29 bottom.
Hulton Deutsch Collection Ltd: 13 top, 26 top. c.1924
New World Music Corp. Copyright renewed. All rights reserved: front cover.
Popperfoto: 16 bottom, 17 bottom, 18 top, 18 bottom, 23 left, 24 bottom,
28 bottom.
Range/Bettmann: front cover, back cover, 7 bottom, 9 bottom, 23 right,
24 top, 26 bottom, 29 top.
Redferns/Max Jones: 13 bottom.
Retrograph Archive: 11 top, 14 top left, 14-15, 15 bottom, 17 top, 27 bottom.

CONTENTS

INTRODUCING GERSHWIN

GEORGE GERSHWIN was a composer who invented his own rules. He drew ideas from popular and traditional music and mixed them to create something completely new. His music was so much loved, he became one of the most popular Americans of his time. To other Americans, Gershwin was the man of the moment, a modern man, a **pioneer** of the twentieth century. He represented everything that was most exciting about America at that time. He had risen from poverty to great riches through his own talent and hard work. He was young, good looking, fashionable, and full of energy. His busy lifestyle drew the world's attention to the glamor of New York, and newspaper reporters followed wherever he went. By the time he died, aged only 38, he was also respected across the world as an important modern composer.

An unexpected talent

Morris Gershovitz sailed into New York Harbor in the early 1890s. Like thousands of other Russian Jews, he wanted to start a new life in America. Soon after he arrived, he married a pretty girl he had known in Russia, called Rose Bruskin. They changed their name to Gershwin to make it sound more American. Morris tried all sorts of jobs, but never settled into anything that earned much money. Rose was strong and ambitious. She had four children, the eldest of whom, Ira, was born in 1896. George, their second child, was born on September 26, 1898. The family lived in a poor area, New York City's Lower East Side, where there were many other Jewish immigrants struggling for a living.

Morris Gershwin (1872–1932), the composer's father, was a small, quiet man, with a great sense of humor.

Ira was quiet and liked reading, while George felt happier out in the streets, playing and fighting with his group of friends. In one scuffle he cut his eyebrow badly, and had a deep scar for the rest of his life. He was often absent from school. On one occasion, at the age of ten, he slipped out into the playground when he was supposed to be listening to a school concert given by a brilliant child violinist.

The house where George Gershwin was born in Brooklyn, New York. The house was later pulled down.

The composer's mother, Rose Gershwin (right), around 1901. Ira sits in front of her, with George in the middle. On the left is their younger brother, Arthur, sitting next to a maid.

American Immigration 1860–1920

Until 1860 most Americans, apart from Native Americans, were descended from people who had traveled from the British Isles. After 1860 America began to welcome huge numbers of new **immigrants**. They came from all over Europe: Germany, Italy, Russia, Poland, and the Balkans. Between 1860 and 1920 about 30 million people arrived to escape poverty in their own countries. The magnificent Statue of Liberty, unveiled in New York Harbor in 1886, became a symbol of hope for these people, and they would stare at it from the ship's deck as they reached the end of their journey. Each nationality or religious group began to set up its own neighborhood in American cities. Many Americans still like to remember their family roots in other countries.

European immigrants arriving after their long voyage in New York Harbor. The Statue of Liberty had been a gift from the people of France, to celebrate the 100th anniversary of American independence.

A street in New York's Lower East Side around the time Gershwin was born. Many of the immigrants could not speak English, so street signs were often written in different languages.

But George could still hear the music from a distance, and it had a sudden magical effect on him. He began experimenting on a friend's piano and soon wanted to spend all his spare time at the keyboard. He could think of nothing except becoming a musician. Rose and Morris were amazed at their younger boy's natural talent, because there had never been any musicians in the family. They soon arranged for him to have piano lessons.

They found a brilliant teacher called Charles Hambitzer. This young man taught George how to play properly and introduced him to music by the great composers. George even began to write some songs in the style of popular song-writers such as **Jerome Kern** and Irving Berlin. At the age of 15, he decided to leave school and find a job in the music business. This worried his mother. George had never done well at school, and she felt sure that without a college education he would never be successful.

TOUGH WORK IN TIN PAN ALLEY

Before the invention of radio and television, people got to know popular songs by buying the music and playing it on the piano at home. Publishers of **sheet music** were making a lot of money. One of these publishers, called Remick's, offered George a job as a salesman. He had to sit in a little **booth** all day, playing through the latest hit songs on the piano to customer after customer. It was tough work, but very good practice.

Remick's, along with many other music publishers, was based in a street known as Tin Pan Alley. It was given this nickname because the noise of all the pianists playing at once sounded like kitchen pans being bashed. George soon became the customers' favorite salesman. He was the youngest pianist in Tin Pan Alley, but he was also the best.

George liked to weave his own musical ideas into the songs to make them more interesting. One customer, a young dancer called Fred Astaire, admired his playing and soon became a good friend.

In his spare time, George began to jot down his own tunes in a notebook. He then worked them into songs and tried to have them published. But eventually he decided that most of Tin Pan Alley's popular songs were rather dull—he preferred the songs composed for Broadway musicals. After three years at Remick's, he resigned and looked for a job in musical theater. He became the rehearsal pianist for a revue called *Miss 1917*. Everybody liked him, and he did his job well. Soon he was made another offer, this time as **accompanist** for some concerts at the same theater. At one of these concerts, on November 25, 1917, a young singer called Vivienne Segal performed two of George's own songs. It was a songwriter's dream to have his work performed. George's career as a composer had begun.

Remick's music publishers in Tin Pan Alley, where Gershwin began his career as a musician.

A scene from one of Florenz Ziegfeld's spectacular revues, which were known as *Ziegfeld's Follies*.

Gershwin at the age of about 18— a hard-working and smart young man. He had a natural genius for playing the piano that impressed even experienced musicians and music publishers.

A LUCKY BREAK

News of this interesting young songwriter began to spread. George was soon given the chance to audition for an important music publisher called Max Dreyfus. This man offered him a weekly wage to compose songs, in the hope that he would produce a hit. Some songs were published and slipped into Broadway revues, but what George really wanted was to write his own musical. In 1919 he was given the chance.

A young producer called Alex Aarons asked him to compose the entire **score** for a new musical comedy called *La, La, Lucille*. Aarons was taking a risk in choosing the 20-year-old George, rather than a more experienced composer. But it paid off. *La, La, Lucille* was a success, and the partnership between Aarons and Gershwin continued until 1933.

An even bigger break was in store. On October 24, 1919, a huge new theater opened on Broadway, and a musical revue was organized for the opening night celebrations. The revue included a new song by George, a lively piece with a catchy tune, called "Swanee."

Right: Alex Aarons, the son of a rich Broadway businessman. He produced Gershwin's first musical, *La, La, Lucille*, at the age of 29. It was also his own first production.

A scene from Gershwin's first complete musical, *La, La, Lucille*. The musical was successful, but eventually had to close in August 1919 because the actors went on strike.

The audience paid little interest at the time. But not long after, George went to a party given for Al Jolson, the greatest Broadway star of the day. As usual, he was invited to **improvise** at the piano. Jolson heard him play a version of "Swanee" and liked it so much he decided to include it in his latest show. He went on to record it, and the song became a smash hit. In one year George made $10,000 from **royalties**. He was suddenly the star of Tin Pan Alley.

Although he was now successful, George was still just a popular songwriter. He wanted to compose more serious music and began to have lessons in **music theory** and **orchestration** with a teacher called Edward Kilenyi. The result was a string **quartet**, which, though never published, shows that he was struggling to get beyond the fashions of Tin Pan Alley.

When "Swanee" was published by Max Dreyfus, the cover of the sheet music showed a picture of Al Jolson. He had made the song famous by including it in his own show, *Sinbad*.

Al Jolson records "Swanee." In the days before electricity, records were made by performing music close to a horn. Sound traveled down the horn to a needle, which cut a minute pattern into a wax disc. Copies of the record were then made in the factory from this wax original.

AN
AMBITIOUS
YOUNG
MAN

George's Broadway songs were earning him a great deal of fame and money. There was little time to think about musical studies. In 1920 a dancer called George White asked him to write the score for one of his *Scandals* revues. White's *Scandals* were similar to Ziegfeld's *Follies*. They specialized in spectacular dance **routines**. *Scandals of 1920* was a big success, and was given 318 performances.

NEW YORK CENTRAL BUILDING

PARK AVENUE, NEW YORK

AT THE GATEWAY TO A CONTINENT

Ann Pennington, a glamorous star of George White's *Scandals* revues.

Far left, New York City center in the 1920s. The city buzzed with energy day and night.

The entrance of the Cotton Club in Harlem, New York. This club became the most fashionable place to hear the great jazz musicians of the time. Film stars, millionaires, and rich gangsters could all be seen here.

In the end, *Blue Monday* had to be composed in just five days. It was not a success. Its tragic story, set in a black **Harlem** community, was not suitable for White's lighthearted revue. Gershwin continued to write songs for other Broadway shows, sometimes dipping into his notebook for tunes, and sometimes recycling songs from earlier shows.

George was now becoming very much a part of America's **high society**. He was invited to New York's most glamorous parties and always ended up playing the piano well into the night.

But George took his next important step as a composer two years later, in *Scandals of 1922*. By this time he was keen to write something longer and more complicated than songs. He decided to compose a short jazz **opera**, which could be included as one of the acts in *Scandals*. In doing this he invented a new kind of American music, a mixture of three different types popular at the time: jazz, Broadway, and opera. The band that accompanied this show was led by a well-known violinist called Paul Whiteman, otherwise known as "the King of Jazz." The opera was called *Blue Monday*, and marked the beginning of a partnership between Gershwin and Whiteman. They later began to work on ways to mix jazz into serious orchestral music. This was one of Gershwin's most important contributions to the history of music.

JAZZ

Jazz is a type of music that comes originally from the black population of America. It has its roots in the work songs and **spirituals** of the slaves. In the late nineteenth century, jazz was centered in the town of New Orleans, where the music became famous for its special rhythms and **syncopation**. Most jazz players could not read music, so a tradition of dazzling improvisation was born. This led to a new generation of jazz **virtuosos**, such as the trumpeters **King Oliver** and **Louis Armstrong**. Piano jazz music was also becoming popular, especially the syncopated **ragtime** compositions of Scott Joplin (1868–1917). By the 1920s jazz was becoming fashionable with white Americans. It began to lose some of its original qualities as it was taken up by more white dance bands. As time went by, jazz produced its own remarkable performers, both black and white. Composers such as **Duke Ellington** and Gershwin helped to establish jazz as a type of music that was respected all over the world.

Louis Armstrong (1900–1971) and his "Hot Five" jazz band. He made many of his recordings with this band.

A luggage sticker from the 1920s, advertising one of New York's most expensive hotels, the Waldorf-Astoria.

Far right, on board an ocean liner in the 1920s. In the days before airplane travel became common, people crossed the Atlantic between America and Europe by boat. The journey for those who could afford it was glamorous and luxurious.

The Waldorf-Astoria
PARK AVENUE BETWEEN 49TH AND 50TH STREETS
NEW YORK

JAZZ IN A CONCERT HALL

George crossed the Atlantic for the first time in 1923, to put on a new musical in London. It was not a great success, but thanks to the earlier triumph of "Swanee" he was treated like a star. While he was in England, he went from one magnificent party to another, all held in his honor.

Back in America, his career took a new turn when he was asked to accompany the Canadian **soprano** Eva Gauthier in a song **recital**. Some of his own songs were included in the program alongside traditional classical music. This was one of the first occasions that jazz was heard at a formal concert. The audience admired George's boldness and the crispness of his jazzy piano style.

Paul Whiteman (1891–1967) and his band. Whiteman wanted to give jazz a more classical, orchestral feel, and this was particularly popular with the white population of America.

Band leader Paul Whiteman was also impressed. He, too, wanted to perform jazz in concert halls. So he arranged a special concert and asked Gershwin to write a piece for piano and orchestra. George composed it in about ten days. It was called *Rhapsody in Blue* and was first performed on February 12, 1924, with George as pianist. It caused a sensation. The hall was packed with New York's most important musicians, **critics**, and **patrons**.

Suddenly, from having been just a fashionable songwriter, George became a composer of important new music. Until now almost all serious American composers had been trained by teachers in Europe. But George's *Rhapsody*, with its jazz rhythms and tunes, was purely American. He described it as a "musical **kaleidoscope** of America." He did not have the training to compose along traditional lines. In fact, at this stage he did not even know how to orchestrate his work. That was left to Ferde Grofé, a member of Whiteman's band. But *Rhapsody in Blue* was a huge success, and in its first ten years, it earned George $250,000.

Piccadilly Circus, the heart of London's theater district, in the mid-1920s.

PARTNERSHIP WITH IRA

George traveled to London again in July 1924, to work on a musical called *Primrose*. It was a triumph. Suddenly everybody wanted to know the fashionable young composer. Over the next few years, he became friendly with Britain's young **Prince of Wales** and his dashing cousin, **Lord Louis Mountbatten**.

George returned to America and began work on his most exciting Broadway show yet, *Lady, Be Good!* The words for this musical were written by his brother, Ira. They had worked together before, but this was the first time they had **collaborated** on a complete score. Although the two brothers had very different personalities, they were devoted friends and worked brilliantly together.

Ira Gershwin (standing on the right). After George's death, he collaborated with several other composers, writing the song lyrics for both theater and film musicals. Ira died in 1983.

Ira had a talent for inventing witty verses, and he now became George's regular **lyricist**. *Lady, Be Good!* also gave George the chance to write a musical especially for his friends Fred and Adele Astaire. Fred and Adele (brother and sister) were by now well-known Broadway dancers, but after *Lady, Be Good!* they became international stars. Fred went on to be one of the most important stage and film artists of the century.

George was enjoying Broadway too much to give it up for serious music. But he was still ambitious, and in 1925 he accepted a commission to write a piano **concerto** for the New York **Symphony Orchestra**. He wanted to compose a work that would convince everyone he was a serious composer, and he began to study books about concertos. The audience greeted the first performance of the concerto enthusiastically— especially George's own piano playing. But the critics wrote that George should stick to writing jazz and songs and forget about composing for full-scale symphony orchestras.

The skyscrapers of New York in the 1920s. As land in the city center became more and more expensive, architects created space by building upward rather than sideways.

Hits, flops, and hobbies

Gertrude Lawrence (1898–1952) was a popular star of musical comedy.

Musicals in the 1920s were expected to follow a pattern. Any show that broke the pattern risked losing its audience. A work's success was judged on how much money it made rather than on how original it was. Gershwin's 1926 hit, *Oh, Kay!*, was an example of the perfect "pattern" musical. This meant, first of all, that it was designed to show off a particular superstar. George and his producers chose the British actress Gertrude Lawrence. They then put together a simple story that included the usual mixture of romance, amusing complications, and a happy ending. The **overture** was used to introduce the audience to the show's main tunes, which the producers hoped would soon become popular hits.

PROHIBITION

In 1919 the 18th amendment to the United States Constitution was passed. It banned the making, **importing**, and selling of alcohol. Many people thought that alcohol was evil and had put pressure on the government to pass this law. But Prohibition was almost impossible to enforce, and many bars and clubs continued to sell alcohol illegally throughout the 1920s. A number of these clubs were also famous as places where top jazz musicians could be heard. Gershwin's musical comedy *Oh, Kay!* is a **satire** about the failure of Prohibition.

Prohibition also led to the rise of powerful gangsters, who made their money through trading illegal alcohol. Murderers such as Al Capone became rulers of a criminal **underworld** that even controlled the police and lawcourts. The rivalry of different gangs led to street battles and shoot-outs, especially in Chicago. Prohibition was eventually repealed in 1933.

Chicago police officers prepare to battle gangsters. The car's bullet-proof windshield has holes for machine guns to fire through during car chases.

A scene from the 1957 film *Funny Face*. The film, like the 1927 stage musical, starred Fred Astaire (center). Also in the cast were Audrey Hepburn (right) and Kay Thompson (left).

Then the curtain went up, as expected, on a spectacular dance **number**. These opening routines were called "icebreakers," because they warmed up the audience, and usually featured a lineup of glamorous chorus girls. *Oh, Kay!* was so popular in its first three months that it sold 57,230 copies of sheet music.

George's next musical broke the expected pattern—and was a disaster. The story was not the usual romantic **farce** but a satire on the stupidity of war, and there were no superstars. *Strike Up the Band*, as it was called, closed after only two weeks. Then, in November 1927, another musical, *Funny Face*, flopped after opening in Philadelphia. But George rewrote this work before it moved to New York and turned it into a hit. The leading roles were taken by the now hugely popular Fred and Adele Astaire.

George had many hobbies. He really enjoyed sports, and when he was not working, he liked to play golf and go deep-sea fishing. He was also passionate about art and collected many modern masterpieces, including paintings by Picasso, Modigliani, and Chagall. Around 1927 he also took up painting and soon became a skilled artist.

Gershwin always remained fit and healthy. He enjoyed many outdoor sports, especially golf.

A scene from the 1951 film *An American in Paris*, starring the dancer Gene Kelly (center). Although the title comes from George's famous 1928 piece, the film contained a whole mixture of Gershwin compositions.

Paris in the 1920s. Although Gershwin did not find a teacher there, he learned a lot about modern French music.

AN AMERICAN IN PARIS

Gershwin left New York in March 1928, bound for Europe. He wanted to spend time working on a new orchestral piece, and he also hoped to find a good teacher. As it happened, he did not have much time for either. He went from parties to theaters to dinners and on to more parties. Everyone wanted to meet him, including great composers such as **Alban Berg** in Vienna and **Sergei Prokofiev** in Paris.

A party given by Gershwin's friend, the singer Eva Gauthier, to celebrate the birthday of Maurice Ravel (seated), on March 7, 1928.

Paris, at that time, was an exciting center for new music and art, and George especially wanted to spend some time there. Before leaving New York, he had met the famous French composer **Maurice Ravel** and had asked him for lessons. Ravel refused because he was afraid of spoiling George's natural gift. The quality of his improvisation, Ravel said, was what made Gershwin's music so special. Instead, he advised him to visit Nadia Boulanger in Paris. She was one of the greatest teachers in the world, and had received many brilliant students from America.

But she, too, refused to teach him, for the same reasons. **Stravinsky**, who also lived in Paris, gave him the same response.

After speaking to Stravinsky, George gave up the search for a teacher and settled down to finishing his new orchestral work. It was called *An American in Paris*. Its purpose, he said, was to show the feelings of an American tourist, "as he strolls about the city, listens to various street noises, and absorbs the French atmosphere." Some of these street noises seemed very peculiar to the audience when the work was first performed in New York. They included honks from taxi horns that Gershwin had brought back with him from Paris. Although the audience loved *An American in Paris*, critics still thought that George's concert music sounded like the work of an amateur, lacking discipline and structure.

Gershwin needed little persuasion to play the piano at parties. He sometimes played for hours, and included versions of almost everything he had written.

FROM STRENGTH TO STRENGTH

Ethel Merman (1909–1984), in her first ever Broadway role, helped make *Girl Crazy* (1930) a triumph.

Below, a scene from *Girl Crazy*. Willie Howard (center) plays a New York cab driver who ends up in a small western town in Arizona.

George grew so confident, with all his success, that some people thought he was becoming arrogant. He spent his life surrounded by a close set of loyal friends and a string of beautiful girlfriends. His letters to one woman in particular, Rosamund Walling, show that as he grew older, he began to think of marrying. But he was too wrapped up in himself and his career to make a good husband.

The future for George's next major show, *Girl Crazy*, was uncertain. The stock market crash had been disastrous for Broadway. Producers had less money to cover their costs (including stars' wages), and the public had less money to spend on tickets. Two unknown young women were chosen for *Girl Crazy*, but after the opening night, on October 14, 1930, they both became stars.

THE GREAT DEPRESSION

After World War I, America had the strongest **economy** of any country in the world, and this time of prosperity was called a boom. Other countries, such as England and Germany, which were recovering from war, depended heavily on American money. But by 1928 America's boom was coming to an end. In October 1929, there was a disaster on the New York **stock market**, when **share prices** collapsed. It was often called the Wall Street crash, after the part of New York where money deals are made. Suddenly America was on its way to economic depression, and the rest of the world followed. Fortunes were lost overnight. Business empires crumbled. Millions of people were reduced to poverty and unemployment. The Great Depression did not really come to an end until after World War II.

Unharmed by the Depression, Gershwin strode on to ever greater success.

It took many years for America to recover from the Great Depression. This picture, taken in 1931, shows a crowd of hungry, unemployed men lining up for free food and lodging. For those who had recently **emigrated** from Europe, the dream of a better life had become a nightmare.

and turned it into a new concert piece for piano and orchestra, called *Second Rhapsody*. It describes the noise and bustling energy of life on the streets of **Manhattan**. *Second Rhapsody* shows how much George had now learned about composing, but it lacks the inspiration of *Rhapsody in Blue*.

One was Ethel Merman, who made an instant hit out of the song "I Got Rhythm." The other was Ginger Rogers, who later became Fred Astaire's dancing partner.

While the rest of America struggled through the Depression, George went from strength to strength. In 1930 he and Ira were paid $100,000 to produce the music for a new Hollywood film called *Delicious*. They spent four months in California, composing, golfing, lying in the sun, and going to parties. Back in New York, George recycled some of the film's music

With the triumph of George's latest Broadway musical, *Of Thee I Sing*, 1931 ended successfully. It ran for 441 performances, despite the Depression. It also won the 1932 **Pulitzer Prize**, a great honor for George and Ira.

Worried and Anxious

Although Gershwin was at the height of his fame, he still wanted to add something deeper and fresher to his music. But people did not want their favorite songwriter to become too serious.

Early in 1932, George decided, once again, to look for a teacher. He was worried that he would never be taken seriously unless he had a complete musical education. Although he had always admired Broadway composers such as Jerome Kern, he was more ambitious for his own music. He wanted his compositions to live on. Fame, fashion, and money were not enough. Gershwin wanted to make his mark in musical history as well. But having written nearly a thousand popular songs, he began to doubt his ability to compose great music. There were rumors that George could not even orchestrate his own work, and that he left this job to his best friend, Bill Daly. A well-known theater director, who met George at this time, described him as "a rather worried and anxious young man."

The Rise of Adolf Hitler

Germany was still recovering from its defeat in World War I when the Great Depression arrived, and the country was plunged once again into crisis. During this period a young politician called Adolf Hitler persuaded people that he held the answers to Germany's problems. He rose to power with promises that Germany could be a powerful nation once again. People began to look on him as their leader, or **Führer**.

Hitler believed that Germans were a superior **race** and should dominate the world. He also believed that he alone should rule Germany with complete power. He was supported by an army of brutal troops, whose violence was aimed chiefly at Germany's Jews. During Hitler's rule, his **Nazi** party was responsible for the murder of nearly 6 million Jews. Gershwin was Jewish, and this **anti-Semitism** particularly depressed him. Hitler led Germany into war in 1939, and found an ally in the Italian dictator, **Mussolini**. By the end of the war, in 1945, both dictators were defeated and dead.

In despair, George turned to a Russian music teacher, Joseph Schillinger. He studied with Schillinger for four years and learned a great deal about music theory. His ambitions were satisfied for a while by a huge open-air concert held at Lewisohn Stadium, on August 16, 1932. It was the first time there had been a concert in which all the music was by Gershwin. Most of his greatest hits were included in the program. There were nearly 18,000 people in the audience, and George described it as "the most exciting night I have ever had."

The following year, 1933, brought more worries. The Depression continued to have a serious effect on Broadway, and George's next musical, *Pardon My English*, failed disastrously. It destroyed the career of Alex Aarons, the producer who had commissioned George's first musical. Another failure followed—a political satire about corrupt rulers, revolution, and **dictatorship**, called *Let 'Em Eat Cake*. People did not find it funny. The Great Depression and the rise of frightening **dictators** in Europe made them want to forget about the ugly side of politics.

Gershwin's concert at the massive Lewisohn Stadium, August 16, 1932, was a triumph. When all the seats were sold, thousands had to be turned away from the gates. All Gershwin's important orchestral works were included in the concert, together with a new piece called *Cuban Overture*.

Porgy and bess

DuBose Heyward (1885–1940) worked with Ira Gershwin to write the words for George's opera, based on his own book, *Porgy*. His wife, Dorothy (right), had already turned the book into a play. Her version was staged with great success in 1927.

George now turned to something he had been wanting to do for years. In 1926 he had read a novel called *Porgy* and thought that it would make a good story for an opera. The author, DuBose Heyward, agreed, but Gershwin did not begin work on it until 1934. By this time *Porgy* was not only a best-selling book but a successful play as well.

Porgy is a love story set in a poor fishing village in America's south. The characters are black, and the hero is the crippled Porgy. The plot is a whirlwind of romance, laughter, murder, revenge, and tragedy. It was perfect for George, who wanted to write a full-scale opera using jazz effects. He particularly enjoyed composing it, and traveled south to Charleston, Heyward's home town, to learn more about black folk music. Most of the opera was written on a beautiful island near Charleston, where George lived in a beach hut for two months so that he could work without interruption.

Willard White as Porgy, and Cynthia Haymon as Bess in a recent British production of Gershwin's opera *Porgy and Bess*.

Left, Gershwin finishing the score of *Porgy and Bess*, August 1935. He planned to work with DuBose Heyward on another opera, but within five years both author and composer were dead.

The cover design of the original published sheet music.

The opera was called *Porgy and Bess*, and combined his skill as a jazz composer with his experience as a Broadway songwriter. He felt it was the most important work he had ever attempted.

For the main roles George chose **classically trained** singers. He was determined that it should be seen as a real opera and not a musical. But the critics who came to the work's first performance, on October 10, 1935, condemned it as a clumsy mixture. They thought there were too many individual hit songs in the score to make it an opera, and yet it was too serious and well-sung to be a Broadway musical. It closed after only 124 performances and lost all its money. George was heartbroken. He did not live long enough to see how successful *Porgy and Bess* eventually became. It is now considered to be his masterpiece.

IN THE PRIME OF LIFE

Gershwin had not had a real success on Broadway since 1931 and decided to abandon theater for a while in favor of movies. On August 10, 1936, he and Ira left New York for Hollywood. George wrote the music for three films, *Shall We Dance?*, *A Damsel in Distress*, and *The Goldwyn Follies*. They contain some of the best songs he ever composed. The first two films starred his old friend Fred Astaire, who had also moved from Broadway to Hollywood.

In some ways Hollywood suited George. There was plenty of money and plenty of time for tennis and swimming parties. There were also many old friends around, including the Austrian composer **Schoenberg**.

Below, a dance sequence, which stars Fred Astaire and Ginger Rogers, being filmed in a Hollywood studio.

HOLLYWOOD IN THE 1930S

In 1927 a new era in the history of movies began. It was then, for the first time, that audiences saw a film with sound. It was called *The Jazz Singer* and starred the greatest entertainer of the day, Al Jolson. The center of the American film industry was, and still is, Hollywood, California. After 1927 the major **studios** of Hollywood abandoned silent films and spent fortunes developing **sound technology**. They had no choice.

Movie audiences had been falling in number since radio broadcasting had begun to grow in the early 1920s. But when films with sound began to be shown, audiences preferred to go to the movies rather than the theater. There was a vast amount of money to be made through films, and soon many actors and musicians, including Gershwin, were drawn to Hollywood.

The 1930s was a golden age for films, and Hollywood soon became the most glamorous place in America.

But George missed the bustle of New York life and was impatient to start writing serious music again. He was also lonely and often said how much he would like to get married. But when he fell in love, it was with Paulette Goddard, wife of the actor **Charlie Chaplin**, and she refused to leave her husband.

In February 1937, George had a frightening experience. He was playing the piano at a concert, when suddenly he blacked out. Doctors examined him but could find no problem. As far as they could tell, he was very fit. But as summer approached, he began to have dizzy spells and splitting headaches. He was also quick-tempered with his friends. Still the doctors could find nothing, so they advised him to take a break. Then, on July 9, he fell into a **coma**, and the doctors realized that he was suffering from a brain **tumor**. A special surgeon was flown in, and he operated on the composer for five hours. But there was nothing he could do. George Gershwin died, in the prime of his life, on the morning of July 11, 1937. A month later, at a huge memorial concert, the shocked public paid tribute to its favorite composer.

Gershwin working on one of his last and finest paintings—a portrait of his friend, the great composer Arnold Schoenberg.

George and Ira board the plane for Hollywood on August 10, 1936. Nobody believed that the healthy young composer would never return home to New York.

TIME CHART

1898	September 26	George Gershwin born in New York.
1914	May	Leaves school and works for Remick's of Tin Pan Alley.
1918	February	Employed by the music publisher Max Dreyfus.
1919	May 26	First performance of *La, La, Lucille*.
	October 24	"Swanee" first heard.
		Prohibition begins.
1920	June 7	George White's *Scandals of 1920* begins its run.
1922	August 28	*Blue Monday* first performed, in *Scandals of 1922*.
1923		Gershwin's first trip to Europe.
1924	February 12	First performance of *Rhapsody in Blue*.
	December 1	First performance of *Lady, Be Good!*
1925	December 3	First performance of piano concerto (Concerto in F).
1926	November 8	First performance of *Oh, Kay!*
1927		Sound comes to the movies, with *The Jazz Singer*.
1928		Gershwin tours Europe.
		Works on *An American in Paris*.
1929	October	Stock market crash. The Great Depression begins.
1930	October 14	First performance of *Girl Crazy*.
	November 5	George and Ira Gershwin travel to Hollywood for a four-month stay.
1931	December 26	First performance of *Of Thee I Sing*.
1932	January 29	First performance of *Second Rhapsody*.
	August 16	First all-Gershwin concert, New York. Gershwin begins studies with Joseph Schillinger.
1933		Failure of two works: *Pardon My English* and *Let 'Em Eat Cake*.
		Prohibition comes to an end.
1934		Gershwin composes *Porgy and Bess*.
1935	October 10	First performance of *Porgy and Bess*.
1936	August 10	George and Ira Gershwin travel to Hollywood.
1937	February	First signs of illness.
	July 9	Falls into a coma.
	July 11	George Gershwin dies.

GLOSSARY

accompanist the person who plays the piano for a singer or instrumentalist.

anti-Semitism the dislike and persecution of Jews.

Armstrong, Louis an outstanding jazz trumpeter and singer. The recordings he made in the 1920s brought jazz to a brilliant new standard.

Berg, Alban (1885–1935) Austrian composer and a pupil of Schoenberg. He became one of the most important pioneers of modern classical music.

booth a small area that has been divided off from a larger room, usually by a screen or thin panel.

Chaplin, Charlie (1889–1977) English film actor who is famous for his roles in silent comedy films.

classically trained a musician who has been trained to perform classical music, rather than pop, jazz, or any other kind.

collaborate to work with, or alongside, someone.

coma an unconscious state, usually following a serious illness or accident.

commerce trade; buying and selling.

concerto a piece of music written for orchestra and solo instruments.

critics people who write about music or concerts. Critics' opinions are usually published in newspapers.

culture the character of a country, group of people, or era. Culture can include types of art, music, literature, fashion, and religion.

dictator a ruler who has absolute power over a country.

dictatorship the political situation of a country ruled by a dictator.

economy how a country's money is managed. Money being made is balanced with money being spent.

Ellington, Duke (1899–1974) American jazz pianist, composer, and bandleader. Although he had very little formal musical education, he became one of the greatest musical figures of the century.

emigrate to leave one country and settle in another.

farce a simple comedy that can be both funny and sometimes silly.

Führer the title, meaning "leader," given to the German dictator, Adolf Hitler.

Harlem a district in the northern part of New York City, with a large black population.

high society the most wealthy and glamorous people in a country.

immigrant A person who has left his or her own country and traveled abroad to start a new life in another country.

importing bringing goods into a country from abroad.

improvise to compose a piece of music, or a new version of a piece of music, while actually performing it.

kaleidoscope a tube containing mirrors and colored glass. A person can look through it and see a whole range of colors, shapes, and patterns.

Kern, Jerome (1885–1945) American composer of songs and musicals. His most famous stage work was *Showboat*.

lyricist the person who writes the words of a composer's song.

Manhattan a large island in the Hudson River that forms the heart of New York City.

Mountbatten, Lord Louis (1900–1979) Member of the British royal family who became an important naval commander and statesman.

music theory the rules and logic that govern music.

Mussolini, Benito (1883–1945) Italian dictator, who ruled from 1922 to 1943. He led Italy into World War II as an ally of Hitler. He was executed in 1945.

Nazi the word used to describe people who belonged to Hitler's political party in Germany, the National Socialist Party.

number a separate act, song, or dance, which is part of a complete stage show.

Oliver, King (1885–1938) American jazz trumpeter, bandleader, and composer. He was one of the first great New Orleans jazz musicians to be recorded.

opera a musical drama in which the performers sing most or all of their lines. The music is just as important as the words in an opera.

orchestration the act of turning a piano piece into music for full orchestra, writing out all the parts for the different instruments.

overture a piece of music for orchestra that is played before the action starts in an opera or musical.

patron somebody who supports an artist by providing money or work.

pioneer a person who prepares the way for others, such as an explorer, inventor, or someone with new ideas.

Prince of Wales the eldest son of a reigning British monarch. The Prince of Wales who met Gershwin was Edward (1894–1972). He later became, for a short time, King Edward VIII.

Prokofiev, Sergei (1891–1953) Russian composer of opera, ballet, orchestral, piano, choral, and film music. He was very successful in Paris and America, before returning to Russia in 1934.

Pulitzer Prize special prize given every year to outstanding American writers and composers.

quartet a piece of music written to be performed by four musicians.

race a group of people who share, for example, a skin color, religion, or geographical home.

ragtime a type of jazzy piano composition, usually consisting of a catchy tune, with syncopated rhythms.

Ravel, Maurice (1875–1937) French composer, who upset the critics because his music broke the accepted rules of composition.

recital a concert with very few performers, or organized to show off the talents of one particular musician.

routine a specially rehearsed stage act, in which the performers usually dance.

royalties the money a composer or author earns when his or her work is published (or recorded) and sold.

satire a type of humor that makes fun of people and situations in the real world.

Schoenberg, Arnold (1874–1951) Austrian Jewish composer, who invented a new method of composing called serialism. He became one of the most important composers of the twentieth century. He left Europe in 1933 and settled in America.

score the complete written or printed manuscript of a piece of music.

sheet music printed, published music.

soprano the highest voice of the five main types of singers. The others are alto, tenor, baritone, and bass.

sound technology the science of recording and reproducing sound.

spirituals religious folk songs, first sung by the black slaves in the southern part of the United States.

stock market and **share prices** stocks are like building blocks of money. Without them a company would collapse. The stock market is the organization that arranges the buying and selling of companies' stocks. Some companies allow the public to buy stocks, and in return these people receive a share of the company profits. The price of shares can vary, depending on the state of the country's economy.

Stravinsky, Igor (1882–1971) Perhaps the most important composer of the twentieth century. He became famous as a young man for his revolutionary ballet music. He was Russian by birth, but became a French citizen in 1934, and then American, in 1945.

studios the Hollywood studios are vast organizations that run the movie industry. They include Warner Brothers, Paramount, and MGM; also the rooms where films are shot.

symphony orchestra an orchestra that is big enough to perform large-scale works.

syncopation changing the expected rhythm in a piece of music by putting the emphasis, or beat, in a different place. The regular beat is crossed by a contrasting pattern, which is called syncopated rhythm.

tumor a growth in some part of the body that can be harmless, but can sometimes spread and cause death.

underworld an unlawful part of a community, which makes its own, often violent, rules. Its rulers are criminals hidden from the real world.

virtuoso a particularly skillful performer who has mastered all the techniques of playing his or her chosen musical instrument.

Ziegfeld, Florenz (1869–1932) American theater producer. In 1907 he began a tradition of comedy revues, called *Follies*, based on an idea that came from Paris. His aim was "to glorify the American girl."

INDEX